MW00909229

Narcoses

Madara Gruntmane

About the translators

Richard O'Brien studied English and French as an undergraduate, and went on to complete a PhD in Shakespeare and Creativity at the University of Birmingham, where he currently works as a Teaching Fellow in Creative Writing. He is also a commissioning editor for the Emma Press, and in 2017 collaborated on his first book-length translation project: Latvian poet Ieva Flamingo's collection for children, *The Noisy Classroom*. His own publications include *The Emmores* (Emma Press, 2014) and *A Bloody Mess* (Valley Press, 2015). He was a 2017 winner of the Society of Authors Eric Gregory Award.

Mārta Ziemelis is a translator and poet, fluent in English, Latvian, French and Italian. She translates from Latvian, French and Italian to English, and enjoys working with poetry, travel writing and all kinds of fiction. Ziemelis earned a BA and MA in Italian Studies from the University of Toronto; it was also in Toronto that her poetry was first published. Her first novel-length translation, *The Water of Life* by Daniel Marchildon, was published by Odyssey Books in 2015.

Narcoses

Madara Gruntmane

Translated from the Latvian, *Narcozes*,
by Mārta Ziemelis and Richard O'Brien

Supported by the Ministry of Culture for the Republic of
Latvia and the Latvian Writers' Union

 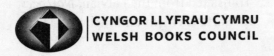

Kultūras ministrija

CYNGOR LLYFRAU CYMRU
WELSH BOOKS COUNCIL

Parthian, Cardigan SA43 1ED
www.parthianbooks.com
First published in 2018
© Madara Gruntmane 2018
© Translation Marta Ziemelis & Richard O'Brien 2018
ISBN 9781912109067
Design and layout by Alison Evans
Printed by Pulsio

Contents

Narcoses

On the left are guys like bulls
You don't need to pull out a red rag
for their penises to take aim
like cannons
On the right are girls like mermaids
and one of them has a phallic antenna
for a ponytail
Beneath her gaze
my face is a red rag
Her hand is tickling her girlfriend's neck
Her red hair is in an up-do
She shoots me a look through a lock of hair
Madara stop thinking about her moans
their range no lower than
a second alto's

✖✖✖

These two are talking too loudly
as they grind cigarette butts in an ashtray
about women at the casino
and dogs off the lead
Somebody spent too much
Someone else drank too much and slept with someone
and ash covers the ashtray's eyes
Everything's going blind
They're talking about infinity and three dirtbags they know
Without context
I don't understand any of it
They aren't children anymore
Thirty-four
thirty-five years old

×◇×

His movements are so gentle
the girl next to him is fidgeting
She powders her nose
Ten times in a row
and folds
her legs like cross-stitch
They're drinking Mad Dogs
and drops of Tabasco
drip slowly and calmly
down the sides of the glass
She's waiting
keeping up an impish grin

✕✖✕

There was champagne in her eyes
the day she left her husband
She'd put in hair extensions
She showed the camera parts of her body which longed to
    be touched
Flashbulbs caressed her figure
On the other side of the wall her son breathed quietly
The boy isn't gaining weight
In the past year he's lost 1.5 kilograms
Click click
She smiles
She's beautiful
The next morning the boy wanted cornflakes with milk

✕✕✕

Click click click
A young man of uncertain nationality
taps his thumb
against a black case hung around his neck
Smoke catches in his eyelashes
A cigarette awaits its final drag
Click
Dirt of uncertain provenance
beneath his fingernails
stands out against the case's
platinum-shiny clasp
Click click click
Please please put out that cigarette
Get your hands off me

And what am I meant to do
with these stares
Hang them out on the washing line
to dry and crumble into dust
Or maybe I should stuff them in the meat grinder
to be processed into mince
then make them into burger patties
to feed the alley cats

❋❋❋

Reddish-purple turkey livers
throb and gobble
You've rolled up your sleeves
an inch above the elbows
Oh you great love of mine
you half-made stew
your arm movements restricted
by your rolled-up sleeves
Hey
Watch those turkey livers
throb and gobble

I put my heart out on the porch to cool off
It had overheated
You threw a pile of shit on it
and put on Leonard Cohen in the background
suffering from
God knows what yourself
The shit warmed up my heart and didn't let it cool
You spat like you couldn't give a toss
and went into the garden to get pomegranates
I tried my best to get clean

8

✖✖✖

The calm pulse of your breath
like the rhythm of falling snow
Shh shh shh
It's damn hot
for mid-October
Shh shh shh
There are no seasons
Your breath
Shh shh shh
sinks into
the half-rotted leaves
Shh shh shh
Nothing changes
It only looks that way
Shh shh shh

I didn't board your train
It pulled away
clacking and groaning
spitting smoke rings into the sky
The train rushed away
clacking grunting its song
tossing discarding releasing
morning papers
nighttime cries
used sheets

✖✖✖

After my sleepless night-shift
Māris promised
to take me to the sea
to unwind
At least his piss-drunk eyes were a beautiful blue
Māris drank wine that I paid for
and didn't take his eyes off me
like I was the one and only
Māris drank big mouthfuls of wine
He left with the mime artist from tonight's performance
tucked under his arm without touching her
He didn't know I wanted to be a poet

If you're not afraid my lips will poison you
then take
take take be bold keep taking
The snake has been defanged
Whitesnake playing in the background

I'll leave
I'll say I've gone blind
I'll overdose
I'll fall asleep not wanting to wake up
I won't even fall asleep
I'll smash into a million tiny pieces
so you can stick me back together

The Devil's so damn beautifully black
he spits daylight into your face
laughs his addictive laugh and prays to God
that you won't ever ever come back

I'm twenty-nine
I don't use anti-wrinkle cream
I no longer sit in the pub until three in the morning
spinning yarns about things that never happened

✖✖✖

Look how things turned out
I thought you were far away
that I wouldn't get to know your family
Look how things turned out
You live in my
ovaries
Look how things turned out
You all pussyfoot around
sowing shit
fashioning hearts out of shit
and then you live and die
in my ovaries
Look how things turned out
Just miserable

Going down Mārtiņa Street
I knew for sure that when I got home
I'd be frying up some boiled sausage
eating it with sour cream
It's a little after eight in the morning
and the sausage is sizzling and smelling good in the pan
Oh Mama everything tasted different in the nineties
Back then I felt your love for me and asked for seconds
Even now I remember the rotten smell of the wooden shack
   on Apšu Street
Back then I couldn't understand why you took so long to
   come home
and why you chose his wicked hands
Maybe I still can't

✖✖✖

In the lower part of the abdomen is the department of
    unlovable things
whose staff deliver missives
to a slipped disc
to a cyst
to vegetative dystonia
Eventually it whacks the whole immune system
with a message to all inhabitants
Love is not proud but I'm filled with pride waiting for you
St. Paul was definitely in love when he wrote to the Corinthians

✖✖✖

An awful dream
Fixtures of the mind
rendered
insanely real
In the morning my limbs fumbled about
You weren't next to me
You appear at night
through pillows filled with sleep
Freud would have something to say about this

I'll go hide under the crashing pine trees
and ask the Devil to damn me to Hell
because God doesn't give a damn about me

I write with small letters
which my tired eyes
can only see when half-closed
leaving open a narrow slit like in a bad mussel
Don't buy those
If the shell is coming open they've been sitting in the chiller
    cabinet too long
Why do they sell those?
I ask
Either it's a con or they don't know
He says
Same here – either it's a con or I don't know
My face is covered in droplets of cold sweat
spitting out poison
It's not the same kind my veins drink up through the IV
The September sun strokes me through the window like a
    mother
Soon it'll all end and go back to the start
It's an old start
Don't tell me you know how to cross things out
Somewhere around here is a crumpled-up tabula rasa

I'm surrounded by throats
rattling on about 'I' and 'me'
I'm standing on the platform
The St. Petersburg-Riga train pulls in
the train cars of St Peter's city coupled to its tail
I'm cold I didn't sleep last night my period is starting
The music group I came to meet
kept rapping in the 'I/me' style
The guy
who called me *Девочка моя* [1]
scuttled silently over in search of shelter
The hotel turned out to be acceptable
The most expensive steaks settled in stomachs
The guy
who didn't talk didn't eat either
saying his *Девочка* had a big enough bill to pay already
Девочка
I came all this way
Come here I missed you
Девочка
Can't you pull away from the ground and take wing like a bird
Я тебя люблю [2]
Я тебя люблю
He sang a French melody whispering in my ear
My darling Ofigenna I almost forgot you wanted to pee on me
The next day he called me and said
Мне тебя нехватало [3]

---

1 Russian for 'my girl'
2 Russian for 'I love you'
3 Russian for 'I miss you'

The smell of condoms
Something a bit like peppermint
Oh you're drinking tea
I no longer have anything to do
with your tastebuds
Another smell is getting in the way
It does a masterful impression of
nocturnal movements

In the classifieds:
I'm offering sex in a pile of grapes
from Rioja
just harvested
before they get crushed into wine

I'm imagining what it would be like
if you took off your warm-up jacket
and took out your hair grips
You've put on a bit of weight
Sorry that's a sensitive subject for me
I was only imagining how you would look
without your warm-up jacket and your hair down
Take my boots off
We'll feel raw in the morning

A rodent is clawing in my vagina
Something you left behind
after the last quick fuck
when you left your mark
after fifteen minutes
stamped into my freshly-made bed
I cling to my madness
Pyramids shape-shift into squares
Black and white peacocks stroll across their roofs

Truth waltzes in four-four
Mothers' hearts stand still
for their scorned daughters

The night is throwing stones at morning's face
and talking loudly
splashing wine and spit
Девочка моя[4] isn't *моя* anymore
Tonight she's growing up and promising
to stop mistaking flying wood-chips
for the children of fire-crackers
And *Девочка* full of determination
saws the whole world in half

---

4 Russian for 'my girl'

Click and it's not there
Click and it's not there anymore
Reason closes its eyes
reasonably closes its eyes
and it's not there anymore
just like before anaesthesia
when medicine flows calmly into a vein
and turns off the hospital lightbulbs
and the doctors' dirty looks
and eagle owls fly in from all sides
and throw a potluck party
Recently the highest concentration of eagle owls has been
  in dumps
An eagle owl pair stays together for its whole life
Reproduction depends on how much food is available
Hoo-hoo
Madara
Madara wake up
How many fingers am I holding up

✖◆✖

God our Father
Dad
Which is more accurate
Those are synonyms
God our Dad
You'll be my Dad — right?
Help me pull together
my trembling legs and wine breath
Help me love the close and not the distant
Give me enough common sense to come back
when I leave
Teach me to love you
Show me the door which will let me get away when I step
    through it
And please make him
give me back my face
I can't touch it

May it be done

He put slices of bread in the toaster
cut into neat halves
only he knew how many
He cracked three eggs
saying that the shells here were harder than at home
His expression changed five times a minute
from an old man's grimace to a teenager
who's just discovered he has another erection
She sat on a wooden bench fidgeting waiting for breakfast
It was snowing calmly outside the window
and the smell of omelette kept filling the kitchen
For the next two mornings they'll eat breakfast in silence
She grabbed onto the image of possible mornings
She stared right into his face
He got embarrassed just like six months ago a year ago and
    before that too
He gets embarrassed once every six months
She marks an X in her notebook

They licked each other's wounds
transforming into werewolves
She howled
at night and at midnight
pulled mornings over her head
like a plastic bag
Suffocating
her throat squeezed shut
by the cigarette smoke
in which he would hide
clattering and rattling
from everything forbidden and denied
smearing himself over every part of her
On Monday morning she crawled away

for good

Her hair shut out the outside world like a curtain
Leonard Cohen played in the background
She cried, not knowing if she was awake
The rivers were frozen but radiated warmth

I'm in a bad mood as big as a stadium
My grandma was a whore
My grandpa was probably a Jew
My best friend has become Italian
and the one from Riga
dreams of stealing husbands and lovers
For a week now I've been trying not to eat
spending the evenings filling my stomach with wine

This is Kenogorgijs
Don't be surprised if he doesn't talk — just act naturally
He's shy by nature
but he's sharp
He sees you
Sees everything
I'm telling you he's sharp
Where did I meet him
Kenogorgijs is from far away
Nowhere in particular
He sees everyone
Kenogorgijs has sharp eyes
He's cute but he doesn't eat enough
He's a vegetarian
He always has frozen blueberries in his pocket
That sound you hear is him scoffing blueberries
The blueberries tint his lips a bit blue
They tint your lips and vision
See?

She loves so demandingly
wanting to prove she isn't a mistake
on the map of the world
sticking her stories into the cracks
of the house's fissured wall
She demonstrates so desperately
that she is good
She traces protective symbols on scarred faces
promising eternal success and immortality
She lets them climb on and climb off
Lets them sweep in and not clean up
She draws an orange on her breasts, hands over darts, and says:
Imagine it's the sun
You're not allowed to hit that bit
There won't be anything to eat

I'm going to eat the most authentic broad beans
Not chickpeas not Indian lentils
Not grey peas either
I'll eat broad beans boiled cold without salt
I'll pack everything else into polythene bags
and stuff it in the freezer for a rainy day

Lonely fireworks show off overhead
drawing
drawing 2013 into being
They are hopeful and expectant
They will have hope they are expecting
I shiver
I tell myself that everyone has their own New Year
at least geographically
Systematically organised into systems
I know a few other people who hate holidays
As a kid I hated my mother for that

Clumps of ash stick between eyelashes
burnt-up tenderness
Why do you think
a woman's face draws black rivers
on her cheeks when she cries

Where can I wipe off this feeling about you
on the walls of subway stations
on the couch too small for two
in your monologues all about yourself
in the endless Arabic harmonies
pouring from your computer's half-deaf speakers
on my plates of uneaten food where everything tastes like paper
on your carefully edited touches
in Milan Central Station
on the train shamelessly dashing at 297 kilometres per hour
under the arches in Bologna
at night by the statue of Neptune when
its perverted dark side comes out

The subway train pulled in like an earthworm
Startled passengers looked at the names of stops
There's a concert tonight under the bridge in the city centre
It's the band that doesn't let the girl sing
She taps the tambourine while the boy wrenches out the
    wrong notes
The boy protests that if they let her wear lipstick and that
    dress from H&M
then the music would fall into the background
So she taps that tambourine in the background under the
    bridge in the city centre
with a God-given voice

You taught me
a slower pace
to eat more slowly
to walk more slowly
to do everything more slowly
without you

The smell of bread is everywhere
The sun scatters crumbs into pedestrians' eyelashes
and warms up the coldest February morning for ten years
We ate home-made bread from night 'til morning

I need so badly to write you down
I feel you moving through my organs with no coordination
panting *fu fu fu* without the *ck*
Every jump is a kick to my solar plexus
You beat out a message in Morse code on my veins:
I'm here and I love you very much
Open your mouth so I can get out

Do you know when you'll be able to tell me I'm yours
When I can bite into an onion so my breath stinks
When I can walk around with unwashed hair
When we can take a bath together and fart
When I can tell you how I lost my money
When I can tell you about my unborn child
One hundred times in a row

My breasts don't get drunk
My breasts stay quiet
keeping time with the dance rhythms
at seven in the morning
leering youthfully into your face

I smell like nettles
That'll mess with your head in December
I didn't sleep last night
I drank and then I threw up
My head feels strange
as if my brain has fallen out
and some of the contents of my stomach have taken its place
Heavy drinking can be a useful prescription
The next day I don't have the strength to feel sorry for myself
In this post-vomit state I admit and accept
that I don't and never did
Ieva said that if you love then everything is easy
My daughter is breathing softly on the other side of the wall
She smells nice
I washed her hair with nettle shampoo
It's Sunday evening after all

Do you know what the very best thing is
Meeting your child's eyes
where butterflies bloom and dandelions dance

Look darling
Here's my suitcase
Oh you can't see
Then listen
What should I take with me
Bread sweets and condensed milk
No no don't worry it won't be too heavy
I've already thrown everything up
No no don't frown
It's beautiful
Pregnant women also
have a solemn clear-out
so they can be mothers

It's already March
Zero degrees on a Thursday morning
Snow is sunning its dirty face
The pavement is showing off its scars
A girl puts on a colourful scarf
and announces
Ships are frozen in the harbour
My love is outside the coverage area

Take my little heart
Please take it and tell it everything's all right
Tell it that when the heart's nerves stop me breathing
it's only to protect the heart
Take my little heart and protect it
My general

A letter to the theatre director Māra Ķimele

If you could find a lover's part for me I'd be very grateful
I've learned to stop smacking my lips
I still remember your warm brown eyes
which I found so mysterious
when you didn't cast me
Maybe now you could give me
the starring role in a show about love
I'll always be on time
Even when I just can't do it

✗✧✗

I'll sort through
the five and four lats tickets[5]
Work out how many I need to sell
to buy a fucking sense of security
The carousels aren't turning tonight
Quarantine
No oil
They don't turn smoothly enough without pain

---

5 The *lats* was the currency of Latvia from 1922 to 1940, when the country
came under Soviet occupation. It was reintroduced in 1993 after independence
was declared two years earlier, and remained the nation's currency until the
introduction of the Euro in January 2014.

I was so sensitive
I wanted you to touch me
It won't affect our loneliness
I looked at the way God made you and fell asleep
Your hand on my arm helped me forget
that I had flooded
four floors of the hotel

I don't believe you love me and I don't believe you don't
Where's the in-between state hiding
As a smart person I'd say it doesn't exist
Either something is or it isn't
I'm scared that neither love nor its absence exist
It makes me feel alone as a single finger
on a crowded hand
not to mention the other fifteen fingers and toes God gave us
For heaven's sake where are you

I want wine and my friend
and my child's half-eaten pilau rice
I'm like a she-cat
wanting everything at once

This love
won't stop squirming to the music
I'd like to join the ranks of schizophrenics
and forgive myself for disagreeing
with the shivers in my spine
I'd really like to step into an awesome movie
Raise my arms in the air and wait to see what happens
Will the man soaked with raindrops run after the plane?
And everything starts again
fifty millimetres of whisky with ice
You are and you aren't face to face with me
I look into your eyes
I'm finished

Narcoses

1992

She crouches down outside the 'Poppy' café
Through the blurry window, chickens on a spit can be seen
  turning meditatively
Mum, I really can't walk anymore
An hour later, a smiling surgeon paws her stomach
His eyes are blue lakes
Here's a little laughing gas: now you won't be so frightened
I'm not going to die
A huge black whirlpool pulls her in
four hours later, she remembers her name
She's eleven years old
A night of brutal pain
Liquid pouring soundlessly out of the catheter
Old women groaning all around her
She's in the adults' ward
She has been in the adults' ward for some time now
The hospital is becoming more real than home
At the hospital, no one listens behind the door while she pees
At the hospital, only women touch her bottom
When she gets home, she cries

1997

Check her pupils, is she on drugs?
Check for lice
Look at how her face is painted
Probably got a screw loose
I was at the carnival at the Art School
My friend drew squares on my face
And then you fell over, drunk
No, I wasn't drunk
I was pushed
Who pushed you?
I don't know
I was running down the stairs
She's definitely got a screw loose
I'm telling you, I was pushed by one of the five men I had
   just escaped from

Good morning
Lieutenant Leja here
Say it, you were raped, weren't you
I escaped
Doctor, in my opinion the victim should undergo a medical
   examination
I don't need to be examined
Please, I'd rather you told me why I can't move my left arm
Everything in order
Why were you alone at night in a dark courtyard?
I wasn't alone, I was with Jānis before he left
Then two men lifted me by the armpits and three men
   followed us
I ended up in the courtyard because I was carried there
What happened after that?
After that they surrounded me and I was in the middle

After that
After that I escaped
That's impossible
I came at two of them with my fists and I ran through
Then they ran after me, down the stairs
After that I don't remember
I woke up crashed into a wall
Doctor, will I still be able to play the piano?
My left arm and shoulder won't move
Why did you wait so long before doing anything?

The police don't believe you
Are you sure that's how it all was?
That's how it all was
Ask the man who found me
He's my mum's husband
How did he come to be there?
Because he works at the Art School
Does my mum know what's happened to me?

Mum, don't cry now
Nothing too bad is wrong with me
Everything will be OK
They'll put me back together in the operation
You'll see, everything will be OK
And my head will heal
Mum

Doctor, I'm terrified
I really want to live this time

Wake up, wake up
The operation's over
Try to relax
It hurts, that means you're alive

2005

First you need to go to the office window to pay
forty-five lats
Through that door in front of you
Ward Six
You'll be next
Have you eaten?

Why have you decided to do this?
I already have three children
There's no money for a fourth
Of course
My husband won't let me
He wants his freedom

But you already have a big belly
Yes
Five months
Couldn't come sooner

The woman who will be next doesn't talk and cries into a
    pillow
The woman who is next lies on the table and gasps hysterically

Relax
It's too late
When you wake up, it'll all be over

1 new message
Jānis: *please let me know when you regain consciousness*

2007

Bend your back into a square
I said, make a square shape with your back
I don't understand
What don't you understand?
How old are you, if you don't understand?
Do you want me to mess up your injection?

Ssh, ssh
Give her something to calm her down
Don't cry, or we can't give you your injection

Where's my husband?
We had an agreement

Little girl, I'm the only one who makes agreements here

Doctor Gailis
What are all these amateur dramatics about?
This is an operating theatre, not a service station

Everything will be fine
We'll start straight away
Can you feel your legs?
I can't feel anything
Scalpel
Scissors
Let's sew her up

Congratulations
You have a healthy baby

In the sauna

Ladies lounge on benches like fallen clouds heaped with rain
their crotches no longer hidden in synthetic underwear
One after another the ladies let out a canon of sighs
They swim like clouds heaped with rain because it's
  Sunday evening
They bought the secret for eight lats

I put on thigh-high stockings with lace tops and knitted
    ballet slippers
I twirled in my awkwardness
It was even kind of pretty
My sauna sisters told fortunes
They were waiting for a lunar eclipse
If you got together it would be forever
If you broke up you'd stay broken up
On those days the moon had a solemn mission
and I skated on a just-washed laminate floor
in knitted ballet slippers
Everything was clean probably forever

Those clouds are drunk
They're mocking me they think they're operating projectors

I'm thirty-three
You can't get drinkable wine for less than seven euros
I'm so used to the sleaze who knocks on my door
at least once a month that it makes me sick
and I'll probably have to sleep with him in the grave as well
This two-room flat in a five-storey building is not
the home of my romantic dreams
It couldn't be clearer that my neighbours don't make love
   at night
Today on my child's Year Two field trip I told one mum
I'm never changing my last name again

Feel me up in fields of buckwheat
Come on dude don't piss here
Buckwheat usually blooms (white)

Saldus is outside the window
Five kilometres later
the ticket-checking lady in a purple beret
gets off in a cornfield
Apples are still clinging stubbornly to the trees
Green isn't green anymore
and brown has turned a mournful shade
In the bus station shop
a man puts back a lemonade
after checking the price and chooses
a half-litre bottle of *kvass* for thirty-five cents
And again outside the window
Autumn is relentlessly erasing colours
There was frost last night
I'm cold and I want
On my phone headphones Damien Rice says
that some things in life
may change
but some things
they stay the same
like time

A damaged, overheated ecosystem
covered by a huge cloud of
calm mild inviting
warmth
That's what they call love
They're spattered with the fear of it

I got lost without the mustard plaster you didn't bring
in a distant bus station
where buses leave two hours late
Getting lost wasn't part of my plan at all
Every kilometre further away makes a mockery
of the minutes I count backwards
to get to you
I think I mentioned that I got lost without the mustard plaster
At the same time my good friend who survived an accident
is posting smiling photos of his travels to distant places
He's fit as a fiddle now
Touch wood

My hands will always be hot
so I can fry pancakes on them to feed you
I'll spread your sweat on a sandwich
and you'll smell like laundry detergent
We'll auction off your obsession with yourself wrapped
    in indigo lace
to museums of decorative arts
In three years' time you'll come to an exhibition of
    my X-rays

You forgot you folded it packaged it up
pressed on an ugly brown stamp
and off it goes

Beside Māra's Pond
(which was also his mother's name)
they talk about how they didn't meet sooner
while two rats split the hot thirty-degree air
with their tails
reflecting the happiness and gentle pace they've shared
since they first met, when it wasn't important
what his mother's name was
or that she didn't have a father

My dear Inuk
I see you rowing
to me in your kayak
with a bunch of saxifrage in your hands
your face hidden under your hood
That day you shyly told me
not to be surprised
that you had left roots on the flowers
The plant is perennial
with a sparse root system
so it will do just fine with me
It's so warm in your igloo and
the Gulf Stream warms
your sea

✖✖✖

Breath like a jammed tremolo
Paris opens up its caring lungs
so that you, darling girl
overlooked by others
can once again take a breath and say
I am the Eiffel Tower people ride up and down me
Art lovers despise me
I was only planned as a short-term project
But look
In a single day you are acknowledged
in photographs fridge magnets figurines from China
by thousands of people who silently experience
proposals at your splayed feet

✖✖✖

Tell me off
Push me away
Cut me off
Cut me up
Switch me over
Bury me
Dismiss me
Damn me
Let me go
Shake me off
Take me off
Throw me up
Tear me out
Cross me out
Endure me
Overdose me
After which I'll
dye my hair with henna
and become a witch

Andris said love doesn't exist

Parthian Baltic Poetry

PARTHIAN

www.parthianbooks.com